DISCOVERING
ELLIS
RULEY

DISCOVERING ELLIS RULEY

BY GLENN ROBERT SMITH

WITH ROBERT KENNER

Preface by Barbara A. Hudson

Foreword by Robert Farris Thompson

Introduction by Gerard C. Wertkin

Art Study Essay by Stacy Hollander and Lee Kogan
of The Museum of American Folk Art

CROWN PUBLISHERS, INC.   NEW YORK

Glenn Robert Smith dedicates this book
to the loving memory of his mother
and also to his father.

PHOTOGRAPHY CREDITS

Pages 2, 12, 19, 20, 23, 27: courtesy of the Ruley family.

Pages 32, 33: courtesy of Slater Memorial Museum, Norwich, CT.

Pages 28, 31: courtesy of Jeff Evans, Norwich *Bulletin*.

Page 36: courtesy of Glenbow Archives NA 3680-8

Page 38: Lisa Larsen, *Life* magazine © Time Warner Inc.

Page 41: Walter Sanders, *Life* magazine © 1943 Time Warner Inc.

Page 42: photograph from *Pagan Love Song* courtesy of Turner Entertainment Co. © 1950 Turner Entertainment Co. All rights reserved.

Page 44: courtesy of Sotheby's, Inc., New York. Private Collection.

Plates 3, 4, 8, 13, 14, 17, 19, 22, 25, 27, 29, 30, 32, 43, 49, 54: Glenn Robert Smith (CA).

Plates 1, 7, 12, 15, 20, 24, 28, 33, 34, 35, 39, 44, 45, 46: Norinne Betjamann (PA).

Plates 2, 16, 42, 48, 50, 53: Charles H. Cloud III (MI).

Plates 6, 18, 31, 36, 37, 40, 52, 55, 58, 59, 62: Ellen Page Wilson (NY).

Plate 5: John Miller Documents (CT).

Plate 9: Christopher Richards (CT).

Plates 10, 23: Joseph Szaszfai (CT).

Plates 11, 47: Lynn Lown Photography (NM).

Plates 21, 26: Tom Van Eynde (IL).

Plate 38: Bjork Photograph (RI).

Plate 41: Jennings Photography (CT).

Plate 51: Johnson & Simpson Graphic Designers (NJ).

Plate 60: Fred Giampietro (CT).

Plate 61: Biggs Photography (NJ).

Plates 56, 57: Richard Genga (PA).

Published by Crown Publishers, Inc., 201 East 50th Street, New York, New York 10022. Member of the Crown Publishing Group.
Random House, Inc. New York, Toronto, London, Sydney, Auckland

CROWN is a trademark of Crown Publishers, Inc.

Manufactured in Hong Kong

Book design by June Bennett-Tantillo

Library of Congress Cataloging-in-Publication Data

Smith, Glenn Robert.
Discovering Ellis Ruley / by Glenn Robert Smith with Robert Kenner ; art study essay by the Museum of American Folk Art ; preface by Barbara A. Hudson.— 1st ed.
1. Ruley, Ellis, 1882–1959.   2. Afro-American painters—United States—Biography.   3. Primitivism in art—United States.
I. Kenner, Robert.   II. Museum of American Folk Art.   III. Title.
ND237.R729S65   1993
759.13—dc20
[B]
92-40230
CIP

ISBN 0-517-59070-0

10 9 8 7 6 5 4 3 2 1

First Edition

CONTENTS

ACKNOWLEDGMENTS

A book of this nature literally takes hundreds of people to make it possible. Although all of the names would be too numerous to mention here, I would like to extend my sincerest thanks to each and everyone for their support and encouragement. Without the help of the following individuals and organizations, this endeavor would certainly not have been possible: the Ruley family, Joseph Gualtieri of the Slater Memorial Museum, John Ollman of the Janet Fleisher Gallery, the Cavin-Morris Gallery, the Connecticut Library of Congress, the staff at the Otis Library, Donna Tommelleo of the Norwich *Bulletin*, Lee Kogan, Stacy Hollander, and Gerard Wertkin of the Museum of American Folk Art, Dr. Robert Farris Thompson, Barbara Hudson of the Wadsworth Atheneum, J. Kevin O'Brien of the F.B.I., and especially my editor, Sharon Squibb, and my wife, Linda, for the hard work and patience they provided me. Also, my gratitude to all the generous people who allowed their paintings to be included in this book.

—*G.R.S.*

Robert Kenner wishes to acknowledge the invaluable assistance of Sue Yoder and Bonita Korn.

Stacy Hollander and Lee Kogan offer recognition of Ann Z. Wrenn, researcher, the Museum of American Folk Art.

PREFACE

I FIRST BECAME aware of Ellis Ruley's work three years ago when I joined the Wadsworth Atheneum as curator of African-American Art and executive director and curator of the Amistad Foundation's African-American Collection.

The Amistad Foundation's collection, assembled by Randolph Linsly Simpson, is a treasure trove of paintings, photographs, books, artifacts, documents, and memorabilia. Collected over a thirty-year period, these six thousand items document the involvement and participation of African-Americans in all facets of life in the United States.

Contained within this rich collection are three paintings by Ellis Ruley. These paintings are hauntingly beautiful yet strange, intuitive works, and have remained largely unresearched until now. Our limited information lists Ruley, described in a notation as a "black folk artist," only as living in Norwich, Connecticut, and active during the first half of this century.

Discovering Ellis Ruley is a book about the odyssey of not only Ellis Ruley, but also that of the author and collector, Glenn Robert Smith, in uncovering the work and life of this artist. A chance flea-market purchase set the stage for an unrelenting quest by Smith to know all that is currently knowable about Ellis Ruley. Both are fascinating stories.

Glenn Smith's identification of a large body of work by Ruley allows us, for the first time, to begin to evaluate his artistry and to place him among the burgeoning group of intuitive African-American artists creating from their imagination. This information also adds greatly to the unfolding history of the contributions of African-American artists in this country.

—Barbara A. Hudson,
Curator, African-American Art,
Wadsworth Atheneum,
Hartford, Connecticut

FOREWORD

ELLIS RULEY IS a spiritual descendant of Boston Throw-Throw, "chief of Ye African Tribe" of Norwich, Connecticut, who died on May 28, 1772. Throw-Throw (does his anglicized last name conceal a reference to Toro-Toro in Senegambia?) was the first famous person of African ancestry in Norwich. He gathered his people in parades and festivities. He left his mark in the chronicles of eighteenth-century Connecticut. His African-influenced aesthetic activity in colonial Norwich predicted, in a sense, the coming of Ruley and his art.

Spiritual intimation of the forest as text links Ellis Ruley to the past. Take, for example, *Cheif* [sic] *Grey Owl + Wife* (Plate 6). The surround of flowers is cut through by a blast of mirrored light, making an altar of the forest, a stained-glass window of the water and the sky.

That graceful translation of flora and fauna into ritual aliveness captures our attention in many paintings. In *Untitled* (Plate 8), streetcars interrupt the green of nature. But tough, strong blades of grass, shaded with energetic strokes of black, seem to make the streetcars levitate.

Honor the ground, the forest, the flowers, the world of dappled shade and lichen tonalities, he seems to be saying in composition after composition. *Accident* (Plate 11) documents acrobatic reactions to the grounding of a boat. But note: it is a *tree* that saves a woman.

Ruley expertly composes his events. For example, *Wild Pig* (Plate 16) shows a boar at bay by a tree before three dogs. The tree upholds five ornamental robins balanced by two more robins on the ground.

Sexual desire becomes the not-so-hidden electricity of certain paintings. Freud has no copyright on what is happening in *Circus* (Plate 40). Many Eves in many gardens tell us how strongly Ruley loved women. He was in awe of their bodies and their difference. But the meditative power of his mind takes over in other works and women simply walk in peace together, flowers in hand, beyond a waterfall, or converse in other settings of repose. Similarly, he sometimes turns off macho noise and combat—guns under trees, a tiger on a man, battling moose, a stag trapped by dogs— and suddenly antelopes are safe to wander over blossoms by lions who relax and nuzzle.

Having never interviewed the artist, I can at least compare him to his spiritual brother on New Providence Island in the Bahamas, Amos Ferguson. Ferguson paints as many petals and leaves as Ruley does. January 22, 1993 in Nassau I asked him why. And this was his response: "I paint from above, what comes from God. I love animals and flowers. Before Adam and Eve were in the garden, flowers were the world. Flowers came first. Adam and Eve were alone in the garden and the Lord said: I give you the prettiest space goin': water and flowers and birds flyin' round. Find happiness in the flowers and the birds."

And so they did, right up to the end. And so did Ellis Ruley.

—Robert Farris Thompson,
Professor of the History of Art,
Yale University

INTRODUCTION

IN ONE OF his characteristic provocative pronouncements, Jean Dubuffet observed in 1949 that "true art crops up wherever you don't expect it . . . whenever no one has been thinking about it or uttering its name." At the very time of this remark, when Dubuffet was contending against the "cultural arts" in Paris, an unknown African-American artist was facing his own life struggles in Norwich, Connecticut. Living worlds apart, it is doubtful that Ellis Ruley was aware of Dubuffet's observation, but his work bears eloquent testimony to it.

It is not certain whether Ellis Ruley (1882–1959) considered himself an artist; it is clear, however, that he received virtually no recognition for his uncommon talent during his lifetime. Possessing a fiercely independent spirit and a richly creative impulse, he nevertheless created in obscurity, living out a difficult life in an unreceptive and unnurturing environment. And yet, even under

these circumstances, his paintings evince the varied emotions associated with a time gone by, happy as well as sad. They occasionally leave us smiling or bemused, but they trouble us as well.

Unraveling the complex tapestry of Ellis Ruley's fascinating story has been the earnest pursuit of the team that produced this book. For Glenn Smith, who first introduced these compelling paintings to me and others at the Museum of American Folk Art, the quest for information about Ruley has almost amounted to an obsession. I recall how impressed my colleagues and I were when we visited a special showing of some of Ruley's paintings arranged by Smith at New York's Cavin-Morris Gallery. There was something eerily familiar about Ruley's work, and at the same time refreshingly new. Lee Kogan, who serves the Museum as Senior Research Fellow in addition to her work as Associate Director of the Folk Art Institute, knew instantly that here was a project for her determined sleuthing.

Over the next year, I observed with delight as Ms. Kogan and her research assistant, Ann Z. Wrenn, uncovered the sources of Ellis Ruley's work. We already knew something of his life through the tale told by Glenn Smith, but we were becoming familiar with another Ellis Ruley—Ruley as a recorder of American popular culture.

My congratulations to Lee Kogan and Ann Wrenn for helping us to understand and appreciate Ellis Ruley as an artist. It is my pleasure to acknowledge with gratitude the work of Stacy Hollander, Curator of the Museum of American Folk Art, who collaborated with Ms. Kogan in the essay that appears in this book. She brought her own perceptive eye and understanding to the project.

In acknowledging the significant contributions by my friends and colleagues, it is also appropriate for me to mention with thanks the efforts of John Ollman of the Janet Fleisher Gallery in Philadelphia, who was respon-sible for bringing attention to the artist more than ten years ago. We would especially like to recognize Mr. Joseph Gualtieri, Director of the Slater Memorial Museum in Norwich, Connecticut, who was the first to appreciate Ellis Ruley's talent and importance as an artist.

The Museum of American Folk Art, which was founded in New York in 1961, has long been dedicated to the presentation of folk artists not only from the eighteenth and nineteenth centuries, but also those self-taught geniuses of the twentieth century whose work is now receiving widespread recognition. Before the publication of this book, the work of Ellis Ruley was known to a few scholars and collectors. The Museum of American Folk Art is privileged to work with Glenn Smith and Crown Publishers to introduce Ellis Ruley to a wider audience.

—Gerard C. Wertkin,
Director,
Museum of American Folk Art

Ellis Ruley and his wife, Wilhelmina, stand in front of their house with their great-granddaughter in the 1940s.

THE STORY OF ELLIS RULEY

ELLIS RULEY'S JOURNEY ended on January 16, 1959. After spending Friday night at a favorite watering hole in downtown Norwich, Connecticut, the seventy-seven-year-old retired laborer and self-taught painter took a taxi home. But he never made it up his steep, serpentine driveway. The next morning, his partially frozen body was found face down in the road beside a long trail of blood staining the ground.

After a brief investigation his death was ruled an accident, but there was a strong feeling in Norwich's black community that he had been murdered. Eleven years before, Ruley's son-in-law Douglas Harris was found stuffed head-first into a tiny well on the same property—the artist's home in a secluded, otherwise white neighborhood. Just like Ruley, Harris had suffered blows to the head, and his death too was found to be accidental—an unfortunate twist of fate, better forgotten. But Ellis Ruley is not forgotten, largely because of the arresting visions he daubed in the upstairs room in his little house.

The irony of an artist unappreciated during his lifetime, then celebrated posthumously, is almost a cliché. In Ellis Ruley's case, though, it was not just the pictures he painted but the artist himself who was un-appreciated—even unwelcome. Yet his brightly colored scenes don't seem to reflect much more than unspoiled nature, pretty, happy women, and pleasant fantasies. They do, however, possess an undeniable power, a strange spell that lingers in the viewer's mind as persistently as certain dreams.

Not long after his death, fire consumed Ellis Ruley's house and much of his work as well. His family and his paintings scattered. But for this book, Ruley's very identity might have been lost, fractured into dozens of isolated artifacts and scattered in the wind. You are reading the result of many months spent scouring the country to track down paintings, photographs, and memories of Ellis Ruley. They are all we have now.

PART I
In the Garden

I suppose that the whole story begins in the Garden. Where it will end no one knows, but that's where it began for me, in a green pasture, under a spreading apple tree, between stone walls. One man, one woman, with little goats grazing, a bull and a cow looking on. They made their peaceable kingdom here, flowing with milk and honey, strewn with sweet apples. Until a serpent uncurled from the branches and they tasted forbidden fruit.

When I first saw them I knew I'd glimpsed something wonderful, and a little sad, and more than a little mesmerizing. This ghostly white Adam and Eve sat frozen in that moment before the Fall, reaching for the snake's offering, staring blithely into the face of danger. Their undoing was at hand, but for that eternal moment, innocence lingered, suspended in slightly flaky paint on a board.

I stood in front of the painting for a long time, just looking. That was unusual in itself, because during the first hour of a flea market, I tend to get carried away. My wife, Linda, and I had been coming to Brimfield Market for thirteen years. Brimfield is New England's biggest flea market. For three glorious weeks each year, a little Massachusetts town gets overrun with overstimulated collectors. It's a frenetic orgy of hawking, haggling, rummaging, and dreaming—not a place for casual browsers. A different field of fresh merchandise opens each morning, and the serious collectors are out before dawn, jostling for position, ready to dash from booth to booth, hoping to beat the next guy to the goods.

Linda and I were out at the Girls' Field by six A.M. We always work a field from back to front, gambling that the virgin territory back there will be better than whatever we pass up front. The light was still dim when we first laid eyes on *Adam and Eve* (Plate 29). I couldn't believe the power of the picture, it was like nothing we'd ever seen. Probably a fake, I told myself, but the image somehow beckoned to me. I asked the dealer, Jim Dickerson of Vermont, how much. "Well, the price was six thousand at six," he said. "Then it was five thousand at six-thirty. You can have it for four thousand dollars right now and now only." I offered him three thousand and we settled halfway. After writing the dealer a check to hold our painting, we continued on our quest.

A short time later, "buyer's remorse" set in. What could I have been thinking, spending thousands on an unsigned primitive painting that might have been done last week? But when we returned to look at the picture in broad daylight, my fears were eased. The more we examined it, the more certain we became that we'd just acquired an outstanding piece of American folk art. The dealer handed us a thick stack of business cards from people who were interested in our painting. "As soon as I put the SOLD sign on it," he said, "everybody wanted it. I could have sold it twenty times." An art dealer from Connecticut approached us and offered $10,000 for the painting on the spot. Linda told him no. He went to $25,000, but still she refused. Thank God she stuck to her guns.

We brought our find back to the hotel room, where I scrutinized every inch of its surface under a black light and magnifying glass. The picture was painted on Masonite board, probably the top of a card table. There was nothing amiss, but unfortunately there were no signatures either. Linda and I were convinced that this was no ordinary painting. We stared at the haunting scene, trying to fathom its allure. Adam and Eve stared back as if mocking us, utterly mysterious.

After a short nap, I began working my way through the business cards, hoping for a shred of information. When I called Randolph Linsley Simpson, whose extensive collection of folk art had been sold to the Wadsworth Atheneum in Hartford, Connecticut, he told me that he had wanted to buy our painting. "I think it's an Ellis Ruley," he said. "Don't you?" I had never heard the name before, but my collector's bluffing instinct took over. I said that I thought so, but who would authenticate it? "Joe Gualtieri at the Slater Museum in Norwich," he replied, going on to explain that Ruley was a self-taught black artist who spent his entire life in Norwich, Connecticut.

My next call was to Joseph Gualtieri. His secretary asked what I wanted, and I told her I thought I had a painting by Ellis Ruley. Mr. Gualtieri eventually came to the phone, but when I described the size of the piece, he told me he doubted it was a Ruley. It was too big, he said. Ruley painted most of his pictures on identical pieces of posterboard measuring twenty-eight by twenty-two inches. Nevertheless, we arranged a meeting for him to look at our painting. Both of us were in for a surprise.

Mr. Gualtieri was very busy when my wife and I called on him the next morning. He seemed impatient, so I began unwrapping the picture without delay. But upon

seeing it, Gualtieri's eyes widened with pleasure. "I know this painting," he said. "I've been looking for it for years. It used to hang over Mr. Ruley's couch and is without a doubt his finest achievement." "Pinch me," I whispered to Linda. "Am I dreaming?" It seemed too good to be true: I had both a great picture and someone who knew the artist who painted it. The museum director had been one of the few to recognize Ruley's talent while he was still alive.

"I first met Ellis Ruley in the early fifties," said Mr. Gualtieri. "He came to the Norwich Free Academy, where I taught drawing and painting classes, to show me his work. I encouraged him to take part in our art fair. Mr. Ruley was short of stature and stocky, of gentle disposition and extremely polite. He had a large mustache during a period when very few men had mustaches, as they were very much out of fashion." Gualtieri pointed to my painting, and said, "That's him there." So my painting was Ruley's way of transforming himself and his wife into Adam and Eve. I'd stumbled on a self-portrait that the artist had once proudly displayed in his home.

"Ruley was married to a white woman," Mr. Gualtieri continued. (I noted that the artist had painted both figures in the Garden stark white, though the man's features looked distinctly African.) "He was employed as a laborer, but he drove a big car and used to tell me with a chuckle of the fondness that blacks have for big cars. He always worked in house paint, painting subject matter that varied from wild animals—with a preference for lions—to bathing beauties, pastoral landscapes, cowboys, and Indians. He had no knowledge of the history of art, and no art training. Never did I see him at exhibitions or lectures at the Slater Museum. Due to his lack of training, all his paintings took on an unmistakable Ellis Ruley look—a primitive quality possessing great charm, always colorful, decorative, and festive in mood, a celebration of life."

So many other self-taught artists had achieved prominence, I wondered why I'd never heard of Ruley. "I was impressed with Ruley's work and I took some of it to New York City to see if I could interest a dealer in handling it," said Mr. Gualtieri. "Unfortunately, no one at that time would look at the art of a black primitive painter. Today, nearly thirty years later, his work has wider appeal, and were he still alive, he would surely meet with greater artistic and financial success. He did not appear to be discouraged when I told him about my failure to interest a New York dealer in his work. He enjoyed painting, and commercial considerations were not important to him. He sold his pictures at our art fairs for fifteen dollars each. The price was the same regardless of the painting's quality. To him, I suppose, all were of equal importance."

I left Norwich with a lot of answers but still more questions. Ruley was an enigmatic character and his work demanded further inquiry. But my search for information proved futile. The painter's name was not to be found in any of the standard reference books. Chuck and Jan Rosenak, authors of the Museum of American Folk Art's *Encyclopedia of American Folk Artists*, told me that they had made several inquiries about Ruley but always met a dead end, and so he was omitted from their book. But they knew his art, which they said "possessed a strange quality, one of adventure and social tension that seem to lurk beneath the surface." Why had his story been suppressed? Where was his family now? What had become of the rest of his work? And how had I come to possess one of the artist's most cherished, intimate pictures?

I learned through the collectors' grapevine that in 1981, John Ollman, longtime director of the Janet Fleisher Gallery in Philadelphia, had received about forty of Ruley's paintings from a dealer in Rhode Island. A relatively insignificant sum of money changed hands, as the pictures had been jammed into an old cardboard box, many stuck together, all dirty, damp, and moldy. "They were easier to pay for than to send back," says Ollman. "A few were be-

yond repair, but once we began to clean off the grime, we discovered some wonderful pictures underneath."

When I called Ollman, he told me he doubted that my painting was a genuine Ruley, but if it was he would offer me $1,500 for it. (Naturally, I declined.) He later told me later of other Ruley collectors, and I managed to track my picture through several owners. After much investigation, I spoke to a man who had purchased the *Adam and Eve* in 1979 at a Rhode Island estate sale. He had no idea who had painted it, but he remembered that the painting had been used as a fireplace screen to keep bats from flying in through the chimney during the summer.

It was about that time that I received a letter from Mr. Gualtieri containing a copy of the local Norwich paper from January 17, 1959, the day after Ellis Ruley died. The headline read ELDERLY NORWICH MAN FOUND DEAD IN ROAD. There was almost no mention of the fact that the frozen corpse had once been a painter. Most of the article was devoted to emphasizing that his death was accidental: "Ruley apparently stumbled in the dark and struck his head against a stone wall." I thought of the wall in the background of my painting. "Stones in the wall were spattered with blood and it appeared that Ruley had staggered or stumbled down a grade where he collapsed.... All along the way the ground was marked with blood.... His clothing was frozen stiff." Something about the article was unsettling: not just the lurid description of his injuries or the emphatic repetition that there had been no violence. Perhaps it was the fact that the story ran on page 22 of the Sunday paper. Or was it the reporter's business-as-usual tone as he calmly noted the 100-foot trail of blood between Ruley's house and the spot where his body was discovered? By the next morning, police had finished their investigation and the coroner had ruled it an accidental death by exposure. Ellis Ruley was dead and life in Norwich would go on as usual.

For whatever reason, the article made me suspicious

PAGE TWENTY-TWO

Exposure, Cold Cited Son Pog Jan 17 1959

Elderly Norwich Man Found Dead in Road

The partially frozen body of Ellis W. Ruley, 77-year-old resident of 20 Hammond avenue, was found on the road, about 200 feet from his home Saturday morning.

Coroner Edward G. McKay expressed the opinion that Ruley, who lived alone, apparently fell Friday night while walking either too or from his home, injured his head and collapsed in the road. His death was ruled accidental by the coroner.

Dr. George H. Gildersleeve, medical examiner for Norwich, said the man apparently died from exposure, although he lost considerable blood from a gash on the head.

The autopsy, which was conducted on direction of the medical examiner, showed that Ruley died of exposure and "excessive cold". It also revealed evidence of alcohol, according to the medical examiner.

Dr. Gildersleeve made it clear that the autopsy showed no evidence of violence.

Ruley's body, lying on its right side, was first spotted at 8:30 a. m. by Richard Johnson on the lightly travelled portion of the road, often referred to as the extension. Johnson, a resident on the so-called extension, was driving away from his home when he made the discovery.

Chief of Police Clarence B. Simpson went to the scene with Sgt. Edward J. Burns and Officers Gerard Keenan and Angelo Yeltz immediately after Johnson notified headquarters. In the meanwhile, Lieut. Henry Hanks notified the coroner and medical examiner.

Stumbled In Dark

The subsequent investigation revealed that Ruley apparently stumbled in the dark while walking either to or from his home and struck his head against a stone wall.

Ruley, judging from a trail of blood extending for a distance of nearly 100 feet, attempted to regain his feet but apparently lost all sense of direction.

Stones in the wall were spattered with blood and it appeared that Ruley then staggered or stumbled in a circle and down a grade, back onto the Hammond road extension where he collapsed.

All along the way the ground was marked with blood and, midway, the man lost his hat. When he was found, there was blood on the side of Ruley's head where it was gashed. His clothing was frozen stiff.

Coroner McKay gave Gager's funeral service permission to remove the body.

When police checked Ruley's home, they found a padlock on the front door and nothing to indicate whether or not he had been home before he met his death. They did remove a small dog from the premises, which barked constantly as they approached the house.

Sgt. Burns and Officer Keenan, in a subsequent investigation, learned that Ruley had been to the Hub restaurant on West Main street early Friday evening. He left the place in a taxi cab at 7 p. m., was driven to Hammond avenue and helped to within 25 feet of his home by the cab driver.

Police learned in the course of their questioning that Ruley had been drinking Friday evening.

Two of Ruley's neighbors told the investigating officers that they had been over the road at about 7:30 o'clock Friday night and that there was no sight of Ruley at that time. One was Paul Johnson and the other Paul Schlough.

Because of the condition of his body when it was found, Ruley appeared to have met his death Friday night. His body, according to investigating officials, must have been exposed to the weather for some time before it was finally discovered.

Native of Norwich

Ruley, a native of Norwich, was the son of Joshua and Eudora Robinson Ruley. He was born December 3, 1882 and was educated in the schools of Norwich.

He was married to Wilhelmina Fox in New London June 10, 1924 and was a member of Union Baptist church. Ruley was employed most of his life as a mason tender, working for a number of contractors in the area including the late Patrick F. Sweeney, Zachae Brothers and Peck-McWilliams company. He had been retired for the past 10 years.

Ruley had a natural gift for art and did a number of paintings in recent years, one of which is on display in the art museum at the Norwich Free Academy.

Surviving besides his wife, is a daughter, Mrs. Marion Harris of Hartford; a sister, Mrs. Delia Story, also of Hartford; and a brother, Harry Ruley of Norwich. There are also several nieces, nephews and grandchildren surviving.

to the point of obsession. I sensed that there was much more to the Ellis Ruley story, and finding myself haunted by the events of that night more than thirty years ago, I resolved to go back to Norwich. I began my search for more information and more paintings. But I soon learned that I was not the first to have searched. It came to my attention that another student of folk art had purchased some paintings by Ellis Ruley. He too had been intrigued by this painter's work and life. I wrote to him in hopes of comparing notes on Ruley, but he insisted that he would not get involved. It was only after I had gone to Norwich and begun asking questions that I learned of his research and found out why he was reluctant to participate. "In the course of my inquiry," he wrote, "I was warned for my own sake not to meddle in the circumstances of Ellis Ruley's story. If the story is true as I've been told, serious wrongs need righting for the Ruley family." He was told that certain powerful people in Norwich do not want certain information to come to light.

Ellis Ruley shouldn't have to be discovered. His art demands more attention than it has received. He wasn't some self-absorbed isolate in a remote corner of the deep South, but a prolific painter who worked in a thriving New England town. Yet it was only by chance that I discovered Ruley in his garden. And when I tried to search for the man who created that self-portrait, he'd already lost his garden and everything else. Had the garden ever really existed? My quest for answers led me to many collectors of Ruley's work, but nobody could tell me about his life. For all my attempts to contact his reportedly large family, I found only one nephew, John Ruley, now also an elderly painter. "I understand my grandfather, Joshua, used to be epileptic," he said of Ellis's father when I asked for any memories. "I know he took a fit one time and they smoth-

This notice of Ellis Ruley's death appeared in the Norwich *Bulletin-Record* on January 17, 1959.

Record of Births in the Town of NORWICH, 1882

Ellis Ruley's birth certificate.

ered it with a pillow. I remember that." But since John had gone to work in New York, he couldn't recount the years leading to Ellis Ruley's death. Still the questions haunted me. I had exhausted every lead I could think of when the letter arrived.

On July 22, 1991, I received a strange letter from Rhode Island. There was no return address on the envelope, and the unsigned letter read: "I am concern about some painting by the late Ellis Ruley from Norwich Conn. The best time to call me is at night." I wasted no time in calling the number, only to reach an answering machine. I began to explain myself when a woman's voice cut in. She wouldn't give her name but wanted to know everything about the paintings. How were they painted? What was the subject matter? How much were they worth? Did I own any? I kept pressing her for her name, and she dodged again: "What do you know about Mr. Ruley's death?" I carelessly told her all I knew. "Do you know of any other mysterious deaths that might have happened up there?" she asked. The temptation was unbearable; I

spilled my guts again. "Do you think he was murdered?" she asked mysteriously. "Who is this?" I demanded. "You're beginning to scare me."

She only repeated her questions, and I eventually told her why I thought Ruley had been killed, omitting none of the gory details. She began sobbing but still refused to identify herself. "I don't know if I can trust you," she said. "What color are you? I have to see your face to tell whose side of the fence you are on." I kept her talking, and the more we talked, the more I suspected that I had finally found someone who had known Ellis until the very end. I told her of my efforts to find Ruley's long-lost great-granddaughter. Then all at once she said, "Mister, you're talking to the great-granddaughter."

I eventually convinced her to meet me, though she tried to warn me about what I was getting into. "You have no idea of what these people are capable of doing," she told me. "I can't ever go back to Norwich." A few days later, when I saw her in person, she gave me a big hug. I could feel the pain in her embrace. "If you are who you say you are," Diane, known as Dydee, said, "then I have been waiting for you all my life."

I have devoted all my energy to determining the truth about Ellis Ruley, and yet I know little for sure. Opinions of his character vary—from pleasant to troublesome, jolly to moody, habitual drunk to concerned parent—depending on whom you ask. That his death was the result of foul play is widely accepted, especially among Norwich's black residents. His house burned to the ground shortly after his death, and the paintings inside it were never accounted for. His family has not received a cent from sales of his art, and many of his relatives will not talk about him. His pictures can sometimes seem perplexing, but much that might help elucidate them may never be known. Even as I began my search, there were few people left to ask. That so few cared for Ellis until now may be the most grievous wrong of all. What follows is what we know so far.

PART II
Portrait of the Artist

In 1847, one Joshua Ruley was born a slave in Wilmington, Delaware. At the close of the Civil War, he fled the plantation and stowed away on a coal boat, "just heading north," jumping ship near New London, Connecticut. Swimming and wading up the Thames River, he came upon a small rowboat, which he commandeered to continue his journey. He kept rowing until he felt he was far enough away that no one would recognize him. According to family legend, he was the first runaway slave to settle in the thriving town of Norwich. He found work as a laborer and soon married Eudora Robinson, a mother of five who also came from a background of slavery. On December 3, 1882, Ellis Ruley, their first child, was born.

Ellis received little schooling, and began working to support himself at a very early age. His parents had four more sons, and by one account, lived at eighteen different addresses in his first eighteen years. The Ruley family was one of a handful of black households in Norwich—all of them indigent. Ellis was a laborer like his father, working in coalyards and on construction sites. Ernest Zachae, one of his employers, remembered him as "a short, stocky man, mustached, and powerful as a jaguar. He was very polite, a jolly man, always a joke to tell. He liked to have a drink now and then."

In 1912, Ellis's younger brother Amos joined the navy, returning eleven years later to settle in New London with a white wife, Wilhelmina Fox. Ellis soon followed his

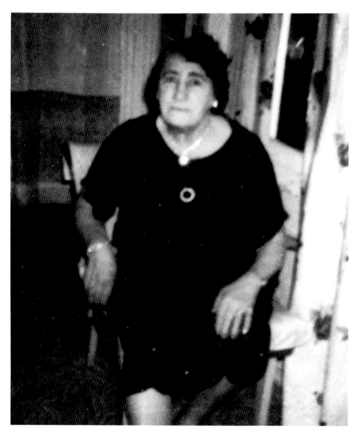

Ruley's second wife, Wilhelmina Fox.

brother to the altar with a woman named Ida Bee, and they had a daughter named Marion. Their marriage was apparently short-lived, though, for in 1925, Ellis moved to a new address without Ida. Not much more is known about Ellis's life until his date with destiny.

On September 12, 1929, fate struck Ellis Ruley like a runaway truck—literally. He and another construction laborer were driving from work when they collided with a truck owned by the Dawley Lumber Company of Norwich. As compensation for their injuries, a court awarded them $40,000 in 1932. Ruley must have suffered the most serious harm, for he took $25,000 of the total judgment. His

1959 autopsy indicated that he'd once suffered a severe blow to the skull, the damage still visible some twenty-nine years after the accident. But the injury wasn't so bad as to prevent him from enjoying his newfound prosperity. For Ruley, the truck crash was a true happy accident.

Everything changed for Norwich's first upwardly mobile black man. He purchased three acres in Laurel Hill, a bucolic, all-white area just southeast of Norwich. He bought a brand-new dark green Chevrolet coupé with a rumble seat (known to his family as the Green Hornet). He got himself a new bride, who just happened to be his brother Amos's old bride. In 1933, Wilhelmina was granted

Ruley's family and friends picnicking on his property. Wilhelmina is second from the right. Notice the two-story house in the background.

a divorce from Amos on the grounds of "habitual intemperance"; that same year, she relocated to Norwich and married fifty-one-year-old Ellis, who called her Tootsie. What may have been the town's first interracial couple moved into number 20 Hammond Avenue, a decrepit, 100-year-old, two-story wooden house Ellis found on his verdant plot of land and renovated himself. Measuring only eighteen by twenty feet, the house, which quickly filled up with Ruley's extended family, was little more than a shack, but he must have felt he was living in a dream. His fellow residents of Norwich apparently did not share his elation. Ruley undoubtedly cut quite a figure back in the depths of the Great Depression. A neighbor remembers him rumbling down the road at dusk, waving to children from his Green Hornet: "All that us kids could ever see at that hour was his headlights, his teeth, his eyes, and the glow from his corncob pipe."

Ruley filled his little home with possessions that still have the glow of luxury generations later. "Grandpa had a lot of old things that he treasured," recalls his granddaughter Gladys, Dydee's mother: brass beds, an old phonograph, a glass clock trimmed with gold. "It sat up on the mantel," says Gladys, "and grandfather always used to say, 'That is a really valuable piece.' We weren't allowed anywhere near that." On Sundays Ellis would crank up the phonograph and let the kids sit listening to old records.

Though he was still a construction worker, Ruley kept meticulously clean. "He worked in mud and stuff," recalls his great-granddaughter Dydee. "And we had to go get two big tubs—one was for washing, one for rinsing. We had the yellow soap and an old metal washboard. Every night after he came home from work, we had to go up to the well, and we would scrub his work clothes and stuff. He'd come out and check on us—if there was still dirt or something in the water, he'd say, 'Dump that water out. Draw fresh water up and wash 'em over. They're not

clean.' And we'd be scrubbin' his clothes and scrubbin' his clothes, but after they were dried, now *that* was the hard part. He had this old-fashioned iron that you sat on top of the potbelly stove. I used to cry all the time, 'That iron won't get hot.' But he would not go to work unless those work clothes was pressed."

His obsession with grooming extended even to his hairdo. He made his own combs out of wood and nails and taught all the kids how to part their hair. (Adam in Ruley's painting of the Garden has a neat white part in his wavy black hair.) When the state came to take his great-granddaughter from his home to force her to live with her mother, Ruley told her: "I'll hope to be seeing you soon, but I really doubt it because of my heart. Do this for me," he said. "Every now and then, wear your hair parted like that and I'll always be with you no matter what."

Members of Ruley's extended family learned to abide by his strict if eccentric rules. "My great-grandfather used to say if you danced to music," says Dydee, "you have the devil in you. So we had to just pat our feet." "He really believed in God," she says. "He thought that his grandchildren should always go to church and get on their knees and thank God." Yet during no part of his life in Norwich was Ellis a churchgoer; more might be known about his life if he had been. "But he used to have a little old song that he sang when he was really happy," says Dydee: "'Ta ra ra ta ra boom.' And while he was singing he was marching through the upstairs, dancing with a broom, and the dog would be chasin' behind him, and we would all be laughin'."

It was probably around this time—roughly 1939—that Ruley began to paint. Unfortunately none of his work is dated, and the reasons for his attraction to art remain obscure. He had an intuitive sense of design and a wonderful feeling for color. He seems to have started painting to decorate window screens: we know that every window of his house was adorned with fantastic vistas. He even painted the neighbors' screens for a price. One neighbor remembered him painting bright tropical plants, parrots, and animals on squares of black masonry paper that hung all over the living room like homemade wallpaper. But the paintings that have survived are more than just colorful decoration.

He eventually switched from screens to posterboards that he put on an easel he built himself. At the town hardware store, he bought countless quarts and pints of house paint, which he blended on a board resting in his lap to achieve surprising nuances of color. He had to let the paint get a bit tacky before it would stick to his surface without running. Humble materials notwithstanding, somewhere along the line Ruley became quite proud of his work. He had a stamp made to mark his paintings ELLIS W. RULEY, and sometimes deployed it twice on a single picture. Although he sold many of his paintings for a pittance, he told his family that he hoped they would someday be permanently displayed in Norwich for all his neighbors to admire.

When Ellis Ruley died, many of his neighbors did not even know he had been an artist. For almost twenty years, he kept his art to himself and his family before approaching Mr. Gualtieri of the Slater Museum. On December 2, 1952, he exhibited several pictures at the Norwich art school. This show represented the most public attention Ruley's art ever received during his lifetime. (He was later described as a "down-and-out character" selling pictures in the back of the Lantern Glow restaurant for $3 to $5.) "His paintings have all of the characteristics of the modern primitive," read a blurb about the show in the Norwich *Bulletin-Record*, "freshness of vision, directness of approach, sincerity, and a love for his work."

Ruley was a narrative painter: he took up a brush to tell stories. Details of life in Norwich turn up in many works, from the town tramway to the waterfalls, pools, and rental canoes of nearby Mohegan Park. Ruley painted what he knew, elevating the everyday to another level. Even when

PAINTINGS BY E. W. RULEY SHOWN IN ART SCHOOL

Presently being shown at the Norwich Art school is the work of Ellis W. Ruley. Born in Norwich on Dec. 30, 1882, Mr. Ruley went to work to support himself at an extremely early age. He has worked in coal yards and construction work for over 50 years. In 1939 he began to paint and now devotes his full time to it. His work was first shown to the public during the "Art In the Open Show" sponsored by the Norwich Art association where it was enthusiastically received by the general public. His paintings have all of the characteristics of the modern primitive — freshness of vision, directness of approach, sincerity, and a love for his work. A series of farm scenes and Indian subjects are among his best pieces. His love for animals is shown in the variety of species that appear throughout his work. Typical of the self-taught artist, Mr. Ruley uses house paints, rather than artists colors, on cardboard.

The exhibition is open to the public every school day from 9 a. m. until 4 p. m.

Notice of Ruley's exhibit held at the Norwich Art School, December 2, 1952.

the subject is nothing more than a river flowing, every one of his pictures spins a tale, usually about the artist himself: his fascinations, fantasies, beliefs, hopes, and fears. Some of these tales take place in imaginary forests filled with good and bad spirits, charged with lust and fear and lurking danger and a celebration of life. Other settings are snatched from movies, magazines, or cozy suburban neighborhoods. The characters in these tales are the forest, animals, women, Indians, cowboys, and hunters, in that order. "He was a painter of events, the exotic, celebrations," says Gualtieri. "He brings to his work a freshness of vision, full of stimulating surprises and unexpected happenings."

Why do these pictures leave such a vivid impression? The subjects and scenes are perhaps a little odd, but not uncommon. The painting technique is simple, even crude. Yet the images strike a chord somewhere deep in the psyche. A sort of otherworldliness is perhaps the most distinctive quality of Ellis Ruley's art. Even his most "ordinary" scenes—landscapes, swimmers at poolside, animals in pastoral settings—feel like images captured from dreams. This effect may have something to do with Ruley's liberties (and, yes, sometimes awkwardness) with scale, modeling, and perspective. If Ruley was less than a great draughtsman, his strength, like Rousseau's, was orchestrating tension in a picture, boiling an entire complex narrative down to a single energetic image.

In the mid 1950s, Mr. Gualtieri visited Ellis Ruley at his home on Hammond Avenue to look at his work: "He had many paintings and obviously devoted much time to his art to be that productive. . . . His home was small and run-down, in complete disorder. With each painting I took from his walls, a scattering of all sorts of bugs would disperse in all directions. Neither Mr. Ruley nor his wife seemed to be embarrassed by this.

"He lived on top of a hill overlooking the city of Norwich. Since the view was spectacular, I would have thought that he would paint views of the city, and I expressed this thought to him. But since I never saw a view of the city, I concluded that this type of subject matter did not interest him." The city was not Ellis Ruley's world; he just happened to work there. But the forest and its secrets and spirits seem to have been endlessly fascinating to him.

There was also something otherworldly about Ruley's home itself: the land is still surrounded by hemlock trees that take three men's arms to encircle, and every-

thing is green and mossy. The children who grew up there remember strange noises and scary walks through the woods to get water; their childish apprehensions were not discouraged by a superstitious step-great-grandmother who warned of evil spirits. Ruley planted fruit trees and interlaced his parcel of land with a complex of rambling stone-walled pathways. He marked his territory in the house, too. Dydee recalls that he added a special room de-

Ruley's great-granddaughter sits on a pony in the 1940s. This photograph resembles the girl on horseback in his painting *Going to Lay Them Out* (Plate 51).

voted to his paintings. "He kept his easels right in front of the window," she says. "His bed was on the right-hand side. And around his bed, under his bed, he had paintings, paintings all over the place. He would sit down and tell me what he was doin' and how he was doin' it and how he was mixin' his colors. He worked many days and many nights on those paintings. He told me that one day his paintings would be famous. I believed him."

"When he'd come home," recalls Dydee's mother Gladys, "he would have his dinner and then go in the back room and just paint. He didn't want to be bothered in there. That was the rule: 'Once I'm in there, I do not want to be disturbed.' He only came out of that room when he was ready to go off to work. We didn't have no electric lights; we had kerosene lamps with the wicks. And sometimes he was in there so long it would burn down. He'd say, 'Bring some more oil in here and turn up this lamp. It's gettin' so dim I can't see. I need to see.' His room in the back of the house had a window with honeysuckle vines and stuff all over. And while he was in there painting, the squirrels and the hummingbirds used to come up on the vines."

"He used to sit there and paint all the wild animals that came to the back of the woods," says Dydee. "He painted exactly what he saw. He used to show me: 'See? See 'em coming right through the bushes?' And it would be a baby fawn and a mother. 'Just stand still,' he'd say. 'Now I'm gonna paint you.' They would only stay for a little while. 'If I don't get to finish paintin' 'em today,' he used to say, 'they'll come back tomorrow.' And the deers, they did."

Judging from these accounts, painting was for Ruley a sort of communion with nature and perhaps even a way of distancing himself from the world outside the garden he had made. Among the few "civilized" influences on Ruley's art were copies of the *National Geographic* that he turned through, stimulating his imagination to transform the deer he saw into hippos and zebras. Everything was part of nature, and the boundaries seemed meaningless. He called himself a "naturalist" and tried to be as self-sufficient as possible. He planted potatoes, carrots, kale, Indian corn, strawberries, apples—anything to help satisfy his family's needs from nature rather than from a store in town. He made pipes from corncobs, even found medicine in the forest. "My legs were bad when I was a child," remembers Gladys. "He used to take salve, when the trees were weeping sap, and put it in a white cloth and fold it. He'd wrap it around my legs so I could be strong and walk. That's why I can walk today." Ruley even claimed to have found a cure for asthma, but he said he wouldn't tell Gladys (who moved out of the house when her children were very young). "She lives too much in the city life," he said. "I'll just keep it to myself."

Ruley did his best to set up an earthly paradise, a wish most clearly expressed (and most nearly fulfilled) in his painting *Adam and Eve*. "It seemed like when I lived with him," says Dydee, "I was in the Garden of Eden. I wished I'd never left." But like all utopias, Ruley's was a fantasy, a painted paradise serving as a retreat from life's pain. "When I was taken away from the Garden of Eden," says Dydee, "the state came and they told us we had to go to live with my mother Gladys. My great-grandmother Wilhelmina [no blood relation] got me ready, but Ellis stayed in his room at the easel." (Even when Wilhelmina left him, he stayed at the easel. Perhaps his devotion to his art drove her away. In any case, her departure shortly before his death threw him deeper into his work.)

Sometime during the early 1950s, Ruley retired from his job to devote himself to art. His ongoing contact with nature became a sustaining force in his life. When he wasn't painting, he was out enjoying the grounds. "He loved any kind of animals," says Gladys. "Sometimes he would go up near the well and just sit. At certain times of the day a deer would come out of the forest to drink. And what grandpa did was dig out where the water went underground. He made a pond where the ducks and all the animals could drink water and swim and stuff. I remember when the first deer came and grandpa spotted him. He was all excited. 'I saw it,' he said. 'I saw it!' They kept coming for a couple of years, and after that grandpa never saw them anymore. People used to hunt all over in the woods, and grandpa said maybe somebody spotted him and killed him."

Ruley painted several unusual hunting pictures. The theme became almost an obsession for him. Ruley's faceless white men in fox-hunting garb have been interpreted as the artist's longing for a life-style unavailable to him. But his hunters are not nearly as engagingly rendered as, for example, the cowboys Ruley so admired. In every hunting picture, the focus of the artist's attention and sympathy is always the quarry—stag, fish, or fowl—invariably pictured at the tragic moment when it has been sighted, hooked, cornered, but not yet killed. The only exception to this rule is *A Day of Hunting* (Plate 50), which depicts two sportsmen walking single-file, the man behind with shotgun poised at the base of his unsuspecting companion's skull.

The series of hunting pictures may be seen as a counterpoint to Ruley's series on Chief Grey Owl and his wife, who are always in harmony with nature, whether praying to the sun or cuddling their pet beaver. Perhaps Ruley thought of the Indians as representing himself and Tootsie, living in the wilderness at peace with the birds and the bees. Ellis's maternal grandmother was said to have had some Indian blood and she was known as the Indian Princess. There's no telling how accurate this name was, but in some ways it doesn't matter. The artist in Ellis Ruley grasped the fantasy nonetheless.

Ruley instructed his young great-grandchildren to cooperate with dangerous natural forces like fire, clearing a field, for instance, by chasing the flames with a stick. "He always taught me I didn't have to be afraid," says Dydee, "because he taught me how to control it. All you gotta do is get a branch and stand there and fight it. It won't burn you—it's your friend." Such an intimate dialogue with nature sometimes gave life at the Ruley household a surrealistic flair: witness the story of a certain black-and-white duck named Bibby Lou. "Grandpa had a lot of chickens," recalls Gladys. "He had pigs, he had ducks, he had geese, and he had a cow. One year we had a real, real cold winter and all the chickens, they just froze. Grandpa went out one morning and saw that they were all dead. Then he saw little Bibby Lou. She was not dead, just partly froze. He got some straw and stuff and brought her in by the stove so she could warm up. Her toes was just hanging there, so he took the razor and he snipped them off and just let her go. But then he noticed the way she was walking—'cause she walked something like I walked, just waddlin' along. 'Well I've got to do something about this,' he said. He took a work glove and cut the thumb off and filled it with cotton. Then he picked Bibby Lou up and sat her on his lap and said, 'I'm gonna give you a shoe.' And he slipped that little thing on and it was too big, so he had to cut it down so it would fit. From the upstairs window, we used to watch her walk to make sure it didn't fall off.

"He loved that duck. Sometimes he would stroke her and talk to her and she'd say 'Quack quack quack.' And he'd laugh. He said, 'I know you know what I'm talking about.' And she'd go 'Quack quack quack.' And us kids would turn around and look at grandpa like 'What's you doing?' Then I guess times got a little hard and we had company that Sunday. Everybody had blessed the table and was all sitting down to eat, and everybody looked so sad. 'Eat your food,' said grandpa. And Ruth said, 'Grandpa, we're not hungry.' We all just sat there. Nobody would eat. So then my grandfather's wife said, 'Well, you might as well go ahead and tell them.' And we said, 'Tell us what, grandpa?' He said, 'Well, Bibby Lou ain't with us no more.

Bibby Lou is on the table.' And we went 'Awwwww.' We didn't eat. We did not eat that duck."

Long after the artist's death, in 1980, Gualtieri arranged for a "Connecticut Black Artists" exhibition at the Slater Museum. "The wall devoted to the work of Ellis Ruley," he said, "had a very special quality of joy and love and the kind of magic that can only be found in a world discovered anew through youthful eyes." Was Ruley discovering that world or creating it? What possessed this man to paint? And what was the relationship between his own world and the worlds he created on posterboard? Based on limited information and scattered anecdotes about Ruley himself, the pictures seem to be remotely rooted in Ruley's experience, but they are also flights of fancy, the work of an imagination given free rein to act out fantasies in paint. Many of his pictures possess a haunting, dreamlike quality reminiscent of the work of Henri Rousseau or Haitian voodoo artists such as Philome Obin. The similarities between Ruley's *Jungle Girl and Lion* (Plate 2) and Rousseau's famous *Le Rêve* are so striking, it's tempting to assume that Ruley's painting is a sort of clumsy homage to Le Douanier. But there are other ways of interpreting Ruley's work that would never have occurred to Rousseau. What Guy Davenport wrote of the French primitive painter in an essay titled "What Are Those Monkeys Doing?" (*Every Force Evolves a Form*, San Francisco: North Point, 1987) holds true for Ruley: "His style is a dialect . . . we cannot check grammar or diction against a rulebook. We can admire its articulateness, verve, and success and can only compare it to itself."

In African folklore, the forest is a mysterious, even sacred place. Animals are spirits, manifestations of a supernatural being with the ability to change form and help people escape their bondage. "Ruley's waterfall paintings," says gallerist John Ollman, "fit into a tradition of African-American artists identifying spirits in nature." Ghostly masklike forms peer out of the churning foam in *Waterfall* (Plate 26), a deeply strange, almost abstract picture. In *Pittsfield State Forrest* [sic]—*See How Pretty* (Plate 32), the running water forms frightening skull-like shapes as two cadaverous little girls blithely approach the stream. There are spirits in these waters. All of nature seems filled with the potential for both good and evil. In African cultures, art has traditionally been considered a way of channeling those forces and protecting oneself from them.

But the forces around Ruley were not under his control. The family was not well loved in town. Both police and neighbors said the Ruleys were "unruly." Their great-grandchildren report being taunted and stoned on their way to school each day. Ellis seems to have endured the racist hostility like a stoic. "I don't think my grandfather was prejudiced at all," says Gladys. "But I do know that the white people that lived around us were prejudiced and did not approve of us as children. But Grandpa knew that black and white did belong together." It was only in paintings like *Zebras* (Plate 38) and the enigmatically titled *Daydreaming* (Plate 17) that the harmony Ruley cherished was actually obtained. "We were the only blacks in the area," said Dydee. "The other kids used to call me a little nigger. But I always got a whippin' for fightin'. My great-grandfather always said, 'You don't fight. Regardless of what they call you, you don't fight.' "

"We were just poor people that enjoyed their surroundings," says nephew John Ruley. "At that time—you think back—what could a black man do? How much money could he make? And where could he live?" When Ellis Ruley went to town, he would enter someone else's world, a world that he never tried to paint. He'd often stop off at the saloon afterward, where he might drink too many Guinness Stouts. His work is imbued with his own awareness of being a social outsider in Norwich, but there is no evidence of bitterness. He never overtly referred to any racial discord, glossing over the issue by painting himself as an animal, an Indian, or, as in *Adam and Eve*, with white skin. Still the tension is there, just below the surface.

Was Ellis Ruley's art a celebration of life or a means of escape from it? Might the pictures he put on walls and windows be windows on other worlds, imaginary refuges where Ruley could hide from his troubles when he felt powerless? Or did he instead revel in the omnipotence of the artist, lord of all he surveys? Another important tradition in African art is an abiding belief in the mystical power of artists. Was painting for Ruley a means of controlling his world, of asserting and recording his values, of becoming a creator unto himself? Was *Mothering Her Strange Calves* (Plate 55), in which deer suck from a cow, an allusion to Ellis's white wife Wilhelmina raising his black daughter Marion? Did the picture function as a good talisman, a way of harnessing benevolent forces in nature? No one asked Ruley while he was alive, and now that he's gone the questions multiply.

"I know my great-grandfather was murdered," Dydee told me. "I also know that the story was covered up and I hope one day it will come to national attention because I made a promise to Wilhelmina that I would see that the true story was told."

PART III

Back to Norwich

Norwich, also known as the rose of New England, has a long history as a prosperous city. The houses on Broadway and Huntington Street are still mansions, but the rich families that built them are long gone and many of the houses aren't exactly immaculate any more. Knowing what I knew, the experience of returning to this town was disorienting. The best way I can describe going to Norwich is that it's like going into a time warp. I felt as if I'd come to Salem, Massachusetts, thirty years after the witch hunts.

"Why do you want to come here to our little town and

Ellis Ruley's son-in-law, Douglas Harris.

stir up all this ol' crap? We're trying to forget what went on up there on that ol' hill and here you are, wantin' to start up all that ol' fuss again." My search for the truth about the death of Ellis Ruley was not warmly received at first. "Look, any other black person in this town can tell you a dozen suspicious stories about their own kin. You're white and you don't know what it's like to be black livin' up here. You're only here 'cause El painted a few dumb paintin's and you think you're gonna make a lot of money on him."

This contact with one of Ellis's distant relatives left me chided but thoughtful. Why was I doing this? Did the Ruley family really want me prying into the matter? What purpose would I be serving? Perhaps this relative was right that it was Ellis's art that inspired me to pursue the truth—but it was also the art that kept me faithful to the truth. I was gradually able to convince myself and the family that my concern for justice was genuine, and they shared what they knew. "Ellis's is a sad story," John told me. "He was a quiet person who stood to himself, didn't need others around. In 1933, he bought three acres in Norwich and married a white woman and bought a new car. These three things caused a lot of problems."

"There was a long driveway up the hill to the painter's house," says John. "Around 1933, Ruley repaired the wagon road so that he could park a car up by the house instead of having to leave it down by the end of the drive. Thirteen years later, some white folks bought adjacent property and began to use the driveway without negotiating with the painter. [These constant land-rights squabbles may explain the importance of fences in Ruley's work.] Ellis's daughter Marion and her husband Douglas Harris were living with Ruley at that time. Marion's granddaughter Dydee remembers when the neighbors moved in. "Our neighbors did not want to see a black man and a white woman with three black children," she says. "But we walked with pride. As children walking to and from school, my sisters and I would be stoned every day. Our neighbor would hit me in the head with car-coat buttons and his sister wouldn't stop him. The mother would never speak to me and the father addressed me as just a black

A gathering of the Klan near Norwich in 1981.

THE STORY OF ELLIS RULEY

person that he just had nothing to do with. He just didn't want us around."

In the evenings, cars would drive up the lonely road and park near the darkened house. Before long, the drunken troublemakers would be outside drinking and trying to intimidate the family. "At night after we got finished doin' our chores we would get ready to get in our featherbeds, and someone would always be around the house and they'd be callin' 'Tootsie, El . . .' And I would want to go look, but Wilhelmina would say, 'No. Don't look out the windows and don't make any noise. Just be quiet.' And they would still be outside calling. Every night. There wasn't a night that passed, not one night."

One day Marion went to get water and found her husband Douglas dead, his feet sticking out of the well. Ruley's son-in-law had suffered a severe blow to the head, but his death was ruled an accident. He was found with just one shoe on, and though police searched for a two-mile radius, they never found the missing shoe. His family suspected he had been killed somewhere else and dragged to the well as a final touch. It was a shock from which his wife Marion never recovered. Eleven years later, when Marion's father Ellis was also found dead near their house and the house was burned to the ground, she suffered a breakdown and was committed to a mental hospital (against her family's will). Now in her late seventies, she remains there under heavy sedation even today.

The story was so impossibly sad, I wondered if it was exaggerated. I sought other points of view, asking people I met in Norwich what they knew of Ellis and the whole Ruley family. Everyone in town presented a different picture of Ellis Ruley. Was he "nice, gentle, a very human person who worried about the education of his grandchildren"? Or "a jolly man, always a joke to tell," or "a lonely old man who drank some, lived in seclusion, and painted," or "a down-and-out character dressed like a bum"? Either the truth lay somewhere among them all, or someone was

lying. And if they were indeed lying, I had to know why.

"I never really knew too much about him," said the mortician who had embalmed Ruley's body (and, I was told, "did most other colored burials"), "only that he came from a long line of Ruleys and they never did too well." In fact, Ellis was only second-generation, but his family had managed to develop a bad reputation in town. I was told that they were in and out of jail, that they had no interest in art whatsoever. One woman informed me that Count Alexis von Schlippe, retired head of the Art Department at the University of Connecticut, was a good friend of her late husband from the bridge-playing club "and *he* doesn't know anything about Ellis Ruley"—as though that should somehow diminish his artistry.

"There were some families here that just knowingly didn't like black people, that was all there was to it," says Ellis's nephew John Ruley. "There is a KKK headquarters in Sterling, about fourteen, fifteen miles away. There were some big rallies up there." The local members call it the "invisible empire," but even in Connecticut, it's not hard to see the Ku Klux Klan if you look. Originating in the South, the Klan was started in Norwich during the 1920s by a Reverend Drake. Back then, hooded Klansmen marched in the town's Fourth of July parade. A strange organization known as the Minutemen rose up to counteract "uppity" negroes during the civil rights demonstrations of the 1960s. They were disbanded after a shootout with police. A former Connecticut state trooper estimates that there are currently more than 300 hard-core Klan members in the area, with another 1,000 less fervent followers. As recently as 1982, the Klan made a formal request to meet in the Norwich City Hall. They had to settle for a rally in Mohegan Park (which turned quite violent), the same park Ellis Ruley once frequented and painted in so many of his works.

One of the most remarkable sights near Mohegan Park is Indian Leap Falls. Local legend has it that a mounted Indian leapt the distance across the falls while being pursued by early white settlers. Most people in town consider the tale purely fictional, but this was the very waterfall that Ruley painted again and again with great symbolic weight. He clearly took artistic and spiritual inspiration from the falls. The legend cannot have been far from his mind.

Nearly all the white people I talked to in Norwich say there were no racial problems there. But one man, whose name was given to me by a "mole" at the town newspaper, the Norwich *Bulletin*, was once approached by the KKK. Sometime in the early '80s, he had voiced his opposition to busing at a Norwich school meeting. He was later visited at home by the "Grand-Pooh-Bah and his lieutenants," who encouraged him to join a local chapter. At that moment, he realized he wasn't the racist he had thought he was. The more often they came to visit, the more "scared to death" he became.

I was getting a little spooked myself, but I tried to stay focused. One day I was in the offices of the *Bulletin* researching the Ruley family. Douglas Harris's death certificate showed that he was only thirty years old when he was found dead in the well, and despite the mention of a "depressed fracture of the skull," his cause of death was listed as accidental drowning. At the *Bulletin*, I found mention of Harris's funeral the Monday after this date. We looked up the Saturday paper, but found no death notice. Then we looked up the Sunday paper, but found no paper.

"We don't keep Sundays," said the clerk. I protested that since Norwich prided itself as a historic town they must throw nothing away. "Sundays are just a recap of the previous week's news," replied the clerk. I sensed that they were hiding something and appealed to the editor to let me see their "ultimate archive" down in the basement. After the editor's intervention, the clerk relented. "All right," she said, "I'll take you down—but only for ten minutes." The paper's historian and I climbed down three flights of stairs to a damp basement. A single bulb hung by a thread overhead as rats scampered among pools of stale water on the floor. We dug through musty stacks of nineteenth-century newspapers until we found the "1948 Sunday Editions" catalog. We pulled the pages back very carefully. "Here it is," I said. "I think I've got it."

A headline jumped out: HAMMOND AVENUE NEGRO DROWNS IN WELL ALONGSIDE OF HOUSE: CORONER RULES IT AN ACCIDENT. It sounded like a bad joke. Somebody apparently had cut out the article and crudely taped it back in, as if to copy it—or destroy it—and then thought better of it. According to the article, Douglas Harris's death was caused by drowning, though firemen who pulled his body out of the well said he "must have fallen in on his head because he had a fractured skull." I wasn't allowed to photocopy the details of the article. "How come you barely allow me in here and yet somebody could cut that article out?" I asked. "These are our archives," was all the clerk would say.

That same rainy evening, I made an unannounced appearance at the home of Ruley's now-notorious neighbor at his home, directly above the Ruleys' property on Hammond Avenue. I had spoken many times to his wife on the telephone but could never reach him because he was never at home. He clearly knew who I was and what I was working on. His wife greeted me in a friendly manner, but he seemed ill at ease. He sipped a glass of beer as I asked him if he thought Ellis Ruley might have met with foul play. "Yeah, I think he was murdered," he said. I asked him why. "There was a welt on his left temple the size of a baseball," the man replied. "We found his wallet empty twenty feet away from the body, and the only thing he had moneywise was a penny in his breast pocket, as I recall."

I found it interesting that he knew so many intimate details of the incident. I asked whether he thought the death of Douglas Harris eleven years before might have been related. "You mean the other nigger living up there?" he said. "He had the same welt on his head as Ellis. I remember my dad talking to our cousin," he told me, "saying something about how Douglas was found sitting at the bottom of the well, looking up, and he had a great big gash on his forehead." This story contradicted the firemen's account in the newspaper article, and raised the question of how Harris could have hurt his head if he hadn't fallen in headfirst. At about eight o'clock on that rainy night, I asked the neighbor to take me outside and show me the well.

With flashlights and umbrellas, we meandered through the dark woods, crunching leaves with every step. We finally reached a small clearing where a child's box-spring mattress lay on the ground, weighted down with rocks. "There it is," the man said when I uncovered the well and crouched down to look. I was surprised at how small it was—five feet deep with an opening measuring a mere nineteen by twenty inches. I looked up and shouted, "Tell me how a guy could accidentally fall in here?" "Easy," my guide shouted back. "You just bop him on the head and stuff him down." He seemed to have a vivid imagination. I had been told by John Ruley that Harris was "a big man, with those eyes that said he could tear you up"—not the accident-prone sort, and he certainly knew his way to the well. "How could they fit a big man like him in a hole that size?" I asked, rainwater streaming down my face. "There's no way," he replied. "Not unless they grease you first."

By this time, I was developing a serious case of the willies. I knew that this man was too young to have committed the murders (he was only six at the time of Harris's death). However, his father may have had some part in the killings. Still, I had a hard time understanding the cause of all the bad blood between Ruley and the neighbors. The neighbor admitted that his father was bothered by

The well in which Douglas Harris was found measured only nineteen by twenty inches and was just five feet deep.

"all those pickaninnies" at Ruley's home. But that didn't make him a murderer.

To cap the evening, I dropped in at Billy Wilson's, a local tavern near Hammond Road. I took a seat at the bar and, as usual, struck up a conversation with a fellow patron on my right. Part of my research consisted of asking strangers what they had heard about Ellis Ruley and his family—perhaps foolishly shooting my mouth off. It had also been published in the paper that I was in town doing research for a book on Ellis Ruley. Word must have gotten around. A large man entered the place, sat down next to me, and immediately began to jab me with his left elbow as he drank his beer. In his hunter's jacket and cap with ear flaps, he could have stepped right out of Ruley's paint-

Downtown Norwich in the early 1900s.

ing *A Day of Hunting*. Though there were seven empty stools to his left, he kept jabbing me until I slid over to the next seat, whereupon he simply moved closer and resumed the jabs. "Do we have a problem here, buddy?" I asked as calmly as I could. "Yeah. I don't like your face." I chose to be a smartass. "Well, my mother never boasted about it. My wife never truly appreciated it, and there are times when I'm not too proud of it myself," I chuckled.

With that he sprang from his seat and growled, "No, I really don't like your——face!" I managed to stand up and ask what the real problem was. "Aren't you the nigger lover from California writing some book?" My breath was gone and every hair on the back of my neck was standing straight up. Fortunately, the bartender appeared just then with a sawed-off cue stick in hand and my assailant was soon chased out the door. Had Ruley's neighbor sent him after me, or had he just overheard one of my conversations? This time it was *my* hands that were trembling too much to hold a beer.

I was beginning to feel that it was time to end my stay, that I'd already been in Norwich too long. Driving home, I became extremely paranoid. The rain kept falling, and whenever headlights appeared in my rear-view mirror, my mind produced all manner of fears and fantasies. I kept turning off the road to let them pass, imagining people were following me. Perhaps I'd heard too many stories about Marion Ruley's complaining that a black car was following her around after her father's death. I was beginning to know how she felt. She used to hide underneath porches waiting for the car to go away. She finally called the police, and it was only a year later that she was taken to an insane asylum against her and her family's will. During her admission she's supposed to have said, "They're coming to get me!"

These and other thoughts were on my mind when I returned to my home base—the Norwich Inn. During the summer months the hotel could accommodate over two hundred guests, but it was January and there were only two others staying on my floor; it was eerie. I opened the hotel's main door with my key to view the usual empty lobby and started up the stairs. As I approached my room, I noticed that the door was ajar. A wave of fear washed over me. I knew I'd left it locked, and the door was spring-loaded, so someone must have intentionally left it open. I couldn't call the police, for I'd alienated them with my probing questions about messy affairs they considered long closed. I crept into the dark room and furtively turned on each light, opened each door, dashing into the hall with each exercise. After looking under the bed, I locked the room door and slid the dresser in front of it. All my bags were open, their carefully packed contents like popcorn spilling out of a pot. Now I was really scared. My room had been ransacked.

I called my wife in California. "Get out of that room right now," she said. But where could I go at that hour? I left my window open so that I would hear any intruders climbing outside. The room's radiator and my adrenaline kept me from sleeping. Next morning I left town without a word to anyone. I drove for hours to reach Hartford and look up the autopsy reports on Ruley and Harris. Ellis's detailed a blood-soaked sweater and severe head lacera-

tions, but Harris's was missing. His case, it turned out, had been suspicious enough to result in a state coroner's inquest. The report was carefully logged, but had inexplicably disappeared recently.

Back in California, I had mail waiting for me. A Norwich resident, Mrs. Janet Peterson, who bought one of Ruley's paintings of lions, had written a letter to the Slater Museum: "With regard to the newspaper item about Ellis Ruley's death—there was a strong feeling in the black community of Norwich that he had met with foul play. He was known to have had a considerable amount of money on him when he left the tavern the night he died, but it was never found and the police apparently did not pursue the matter." After Ellis's death, his Green Hornet car disappeared; a city judge was later seen driving the car around town. Ellis's house was burned to the ground within six months of his death. Fifty or sixty paintings

Downtown Norwich in 1959.

vanished, as did Ruley's costly "treasures." His nephew Harry Ruley had told me that I'd "get into a mystery" if I uncovered what happened to Ruley's art and property. He said he once paid a lawyer $1,200 to pursue it, but the case was not handled properly: "Very prominent people in Norwich are involved in the cover-up. There is money at stake." There is no accurate account of the number of pictures Ellis Ruley painted. Though I've searched exhaustively, there are quite possibly additional undiscovered Ruleys out there somewhere.

"I can tell you how the story goes," Dydee told me. "What caused so much violence between the neighbors and Ellis Walter Ruley was that his neighbor's wife was pregnant and she was going to have a baby and my grandfather had a car. The old man came to my grandfather and asked him to rush his wife to the hospital. My grandfather could not get ready in time and when he got there, the wife had lost the baby. And from then on there was just hard feelings between the two of them. And that's what my grandparents told me, 'cause I wanted to know why they were so mean. And this is what they told me."

Dydee's mother, Gladys, recounted Ellis's telling the neighbor over and over that he didn't own the road, that it was a public road and all were free to walk on it. "I don't have the slightest idea who killed my grandfather," says Gladys, "but I say it could have been [the neighbor] 'cause he hated us. He would tell my grandfather, 'I will do everything in my power to get your land because I want to own from the bottom of the road all the way clear around.' He tried to buy the land, because he's got another house, but my father said, 'No, I'll never sell it to you.' So I say he has a lot to do with the killing."

"Ellis was down there to the bar," says John Ruley. "He drank many beers, and he got out of the taxi. Something could have been set up. I don't know, but it would have been very easy to do. He was an old man and what could he do? They could get away with it. As far as the Po-

lice Department, I don't think they wanted that scandal or so-called thing on their talent of knowledge, because they always wore a lily-white shoe up here. So many atrocities were handed down to the people here, it's a shame how this government can't realize what it is really doin' for the people."

"What you're saying is why didn't the police investigate it further?" said Ruley's embalmer, Krodel, when I asked him about the missing coroner's report. "You find somebody who's a recluse like that and back in those days if they didn't have any witness or, you know, it seems back in those days they just didn't investigate things like that. I wondered why myself, but sometimes they just looked the other way."

"He was a fond old gentleman," another townsperson said of Ruley. "He was living at the time and to the fullest. The only time he went to town, you know, drinking or anything was when he got his Social Security check. Usually on the thirtieth or the first." The neighbor said he and his father were the first to discover the body. He also remembered details of the incident—notably Ruley's empty wallet, which is not mentioned in any newspaper or other reports, and the single penny in Ruley's pocket.

I am no private detective. Through the whole affair, I kept asking myself, What are the chances of somebody like me getting involved in all this? I could have been like the man who, while traveling to Norwich on business in 1959, became intrigued with some of Ruley's painted screens. He found the painter "in a shack in desperate circumstances" with the house full of paintings "of the primitive kind." At the time, all of Ellis's pictures were reduced from $15 to just $5. He was sorry for the painter, but didn't care for his work and decided to see him again the next year. (Of course, Ellis was dead by then.) For me, it was the art of Ellis Ruley that put me onto this mystery in the first place. I remain fascinated by Ruley's need to make art despite everything going on around him. He was at times in a living hell. What possessed this man to paint?

When asked who the characters depicted in Ruley's art were, Dydee replied, more profoundly than she may know, "I believe the people in his paintings were somewhat of his imagination or people he might have met, people that he might have saw." I was reminded of another writer's observation that "to a profound extent, an artist *is* his art, his craft, his medium. Art is not merely something he uses to clarify his position or to give point to his vision of life, but is, rather, the very substance of who he is and what he wants to say."

CODA

Up in Smoke

On my last trip to Norwich, I visited the Maplewood Cemetery. I found Ellis Ruley's grave, marked only by a three-inch stone numbered "185." Douglas Harris was buried nearby under a larger headstone, complete with a little enamel cameo portrait of the deceased. Harris's likeness, though, had been deliberately hacked away, so that his face—and race—were obliterated.

Many questions about the Ruleys remain not only unanswered but unasked. Those paintings that have survived speak a kind of truth by recording the facts of life in Ruley's garden. They testify to an understanding between a family and nature: flesh and blood and earth, air, and fire living in harmony. Though the pact was broken, blood was spilled on earth, and flames consumed everything, Ruley's children—paintings and people—still help keep the faith.

"My great-grandfather used to go have to burn the lots off," remembers Dydee. "After school he would tell us to change our clothes because we had work to do. We would go down to the lower lot, down to where his body was found, and he would take the match and set the grass on fire. And then he would walk over to the big pine tree and

The foundation is all that's left of Ellis Ruley's house.

take a big branch off and hand it to us and tell us to 'control the fire.' And how we controlled the fire was to take a branch and beat the fire back while the grass was burnin'—so it wouldn't go over to [the neighbor]'s, because grandpa didn't want any problems from them. He said he had enough problems already.

"When the fire is burnin' and you're standin' there and you're watchin' the fire startin' to rise, and as you take that branch, and you start to come down on it, the fire just smooths itself right out and it starts backin' off and gatherin' itself together. And you have control of it. Smoke's risin' up in the sky and the field is turnin' black. You gotta try it one time. They have fire trucks out here with water shootin' foam, and I look up and I say, 'Boy, how stupid they are.' All you gotta do is go get a branch and stand there and fight it. Fire won't hurt you. It's your friend. That's what it is."

—Glenn Robert Smith
with Robert Kenner

Figure 1. "Beaver in canoe. Canoe and camp inspection is included in the daily routine of the beaver," reads the caption to photograph of Grey Owl in *Men of the Last Frontier*. Grey Owl's relationships with nature included bringing beavers into his own home. Photographs documenting the friendship formed the basis of several paintings by Ruley.

FILTERED IMAGES: THE ART OF ELLIS RULEY

ELLIS RULEY WAS not a visionary, as the term is used today. His dreams did not include space travel or religion knocking at every door; they did not speak loudly of the experiences of a whole community. Ruley's dreams were personal, stories of heroism, peace, beauty, and freedom that were firmly rooted in his own time and place as he understood it from his home in Norwich, Connecticut.

Ellis Ruley was an African-American man living in the often hostile environment of the white community of Norwich from the late nineteenth century through the first half of the twentieth. He owned his own home, property, and car, allowing him an independence that seems to have at once amused and goaded his neighbors. Ruley lived during a period that encompassed the Great Depression, the stresses of wartime, and the pre–Civil Rights era. Because he was subject to the historical forces around him, Ruley was unable to

Figure 2. Cover model Chili Williams appeared in _Life_ magazine on September 27 and November 22, 1943, wearing her clown dot two-piece bathing suit. This photograph of Chili Williams may have been the inspiration for Ruley's _Parrot Girl_ (Plate 62).

attain in reality the freedom he internalized in fantasy. Through his narrative and episodic paintings, he reveals an idealized world of his own imagination filled with romantic, escapist adventures and bubbly women that enhanced and transformed his life.

Popular culture has traditionally influenced self-taught artists, and Ruley's paintings, in particular, provide a mirror reflection of the times in which he lived. The flood of books, magazines, newspapers, movies, radio, and television that reaches even the most remote areas of the United States has had a major impact on the work of self-taught artists. The images found in these media have a double value: they provide both evocative subject matter for interpretation and examples of forms for copying, alteration, and elaboration.

There is a long tradition of artists using source material as inspiration in their own work. During the eighteenth and nineteenth centuries, artisan painters worked from widely circulated prints based on the paintings of such European court painters as Sir Peter Lely (1618–1680) and Sir Godfrey Kneller (1646–1723). Pose, costume, and gesture were formal compositional elements that these artists borrowed and incorporated into their paintings of the new middle class that was rapidly developing following the American Revolution. Genre painters of the mid- and late nineteenth century drew their subject matter from images in popular magazines and prints by Currier and Ives. The well-known painting _The Quilting Party_, for example, was based on a woodcut illustration published in _Gleason's Pictorial_ in 1854. Edward Hicks, the nineteenth-century Quaker minister whose approximately sixty _Peaceable Kingdom_ paintings are among the most cherished folk paintings, used printed sources for some of the groupings of people and animals found in his works. These sources included engravings based on the work of renowned artists such as Benjamin West and Richard Westall.

Grandma Moses (Anna Robertson Moses), perhaps the most widely recognized American folk painter of the first half of this century, planned her compositions by reassembling the images she culled from newspapers and magazines. Contemporary self-taught painters Eddie Arning and William Hawkins have continued the tradition in the latter part of the century. Arning used magazine advertisements as the basis for his psychologically complex crayon and oil pastel drawings, and Hawkins used magazine and newspaper pictures that he stored in an old battered suitcase.

This same reliance on published images is crucial to understanding the paintings of Ellis Ruley. The sense of familiarity one feels upon first viewing his work stems from his use of images and archetypes imprinted upon our collective consciousness through common, popular experience. Though the sources of Ruley's imagery were not known at the advent of our consideration of the artist's work, intensive research at the Museum of American Folk Art in New York City has resulted in the discovery of an exciting wealth of source material. *Life* magazine, *National Geographic*, the New York *Daily News*, and other publications of the day formed the basis of Ruley's contact with the larger world around him. Pinup girls, romantic leading men, cowboys, and other popular heroes of the 1940s and '50s—morale boosters that diverted both the American public and servicemen from the unremitting seriousness of war—must have provided Ruley with the raw material he needed to create a rich fantasy world where he played the leading role. *Parrot Girl* (Plate 62), for instance, is probably a depiction of cover girl Chili Williams, whose bright smile and polkadot two-piece bathing suit graced the pages of *Life* on September 27, 1943, prompting a response from 100,000 fans. We can imagine that in Ruley's world, her smile was for him alone (figure 2).

Clearly, visual idioms of the day repeatedly influenced the colors, patterns, and thematic choices that characterize Ruley's paintings. Most important, perhaps, was Ruley's conversance with a series of books written and illustrated by Chief Grey Owl, a self-styled environmentalist who spent years in the Canadian north. "Grey Owl" was the assumed identity of Archibald Belaney, an Englishman born and raised by two maiden aunts. At the age of eighteen, after a series of family troubles, he left England for Ontario and reinvented himself as Chief Grey Owl, a half-breed born of a Scottish father and Indian mother. After falling in love with a beautiful Iroquois girl named Anahareo, the self-fashioned Ojibway Indian spent years in the Canadian wilderness living as a trapper, riverman, and forest ranger. Existing in harmony with his natural surroundings, he devoted much of his energy to the protection of wild animals and became an impassioned environmentalist. He achieved fame and self-validation through his publications and lectures in England and the United States (figure 3).

Figure 3. Photograph of Grey Owl in *Tales of an Empty Cabin* by Grey Owl (New York: Dodd Mead & Co., 1937). His philosophy, based on tolerance and respect for all living creatures, had a profound effect on Ellis Ruley's art.

The idea of transformation and escape from unpleasant reality to the freedom of the outdoors, as illustrated in Grey Owl's writings, became a personal symbol for Ellis Ruley. In his own quest to break the bonds of his surroundings, he assimilated Grey Owl's experiences and used them as the vehicle for the exploration of his own yearnings.

Ruley's identification with Grey Owl is a natural consequence of his own search for reinvention. According to his biographer, Lovat Dickson, when Belaney lectured, he told "with his deep and thrilling voice that someplace there was a land where life could begin again, a place where the screams of demented dictators could not reach, where the air was fresh and not stagnant with the fumes of industry, where the wild animals and men could co-exist without murderous intent." The impact of these words and the hope they conveyed must have made even the impossible seem within reach. For Ruley, they gave voice to his own unspoken philosophy. To complete his identification with Grey Owl, Ruley's own interracial marriage to a white woman seemed to brand him as a maverick, too, and cemented the bond he felt with the "Indian" hero.

Grey Owl kept a comprehensive visual record of the fairy-tale existence he invented, and photographs and drawings from his books obviously inspired a number of Ruley's paintings. Grey Owl portrays himself and his wife in a direct and sympathetic relationship with nature. Their pets are woodland creatures, their lives a symbiotic coexistence with

Figure 4. *Once He Saw a Silver-Coated Lynx* is a sketch by Grey Owl from *Sajo and the Beaver People*. Ruley found an apt symbol of himself in Grey Owl's illustration of the lynx.

their environment. Ruley's paintings of moose peacefully reflected in water, beavers, and other creatures bear direct similarities to images in the books. Grey Owl's sketch of a lynx is adopted as Ruley's symbol of himself, appearing several times throughout his paintings (figure 4). Ruley's paintings of waterfalls and other natural formations may well have been derived at least partly from his own surroundings, as has been suggested, but may also be studies drawn from the Grey Owl literature. At least one painting is based on Grey Owl's autobiography. *McNoil's Famous Horse* (Plate 19) was clearly born of Grey Owl's claim that his father was a Scotsman named McNeill who had once appeared in Buffalo Bill's Wild West Show in the South.

Other paintings are informed by illustrations and text material in the Grey Owl books including *Mrs. Grey Owl and Her Pet Beaver* (Plate 7), *Cheif* [sic] *Grey Owl and Wife* (Plate 42; figure 1), and *Cheif* [sic] *Grey Owl + Wife* (Plate 6). Grey Owl's philosophy of tolerance and caring for all living creatures is reiterated in Ruley's own words on the back of *Cheif* [sic] *Grey Owl + Wife* . In the depiction, the couple are praying, their arms outstretched toward the open sky, their discarded gun and two animal leg traps set on the ground. On the reverse side of the painting near the top in faint cursive script, the following words appear: "Cheif [sic] Grey Owl + Wife/ Praying outh [out] the [they] said/ Kill no more—animal only to Eat."

In an article titled "Why We Need Heroes to Be Heroic" (*Journal of Popular Culture*, fall 1988), Professor of Sociology Ian M. Taplin of Wake Forest University writes, "Recognizing our inability to significantly alter our lot, we embark upon inner journeys of gratification, punctuated by periodic escape attempts which alleviate the accumulated tensions of our working lives." Perhaps Ruley's search for heroes led him to the cowboy as his metaphor for the American dream. As conqueror of the West, righter of wrongs, avenger of the weak, the cowboy was an immediately accessible symbol from television, radio, and magazines. The Roy Rogers films

(1930–1942) and television series (1951–1957) may have inspired Ruley to paint *Lone Ranger* (Plate 18). Though named after the well-known cowboy avenger, this painting actually portrayed, not the eponymous television hero, but Roy Rogers, the "King of the Cowboys." On July 23, 1948, Rogers was featured on the cover of *Life* in virtually the same pose as the figure in Ruley's painting (figure 5). The trappings on the horse are identical to those adorning Rogers's famous golden palomino stallion, but Ruley's horse is white, closer in color to the Lone Ranger's Silver. In combining characteristics of America's two leading cowboy figures, Ruley pays tribute to the cowboy as America's savior—confident, competent, morally strong, friendly—and identifies himself with the heroic attributes of the cowboy. Probably adding to Ruley's interest in Roy Rogers was the deep religious commitment the Cowboy and his wife Dale Evans shared in combating racism.

Wild Bill Elliott was another Western film star whom Ruley admired and portrayed in his paintings. *Greening King Billy and Thunder* (Plate 1) refers to this burly leading man of the 1920s who appeared in many second-feature Westerns and mysteries. Elliott and his horse Thunder also appeared in Westerns in the late 1940s and '50s.

Cowboys, outlaws, heroes, and antiheroes were only one aspect of Ruley's inner life as artistically expressed. Remote and exotic lands, introduced into the popular imagination through movies and magazines such as *National Geographic*, figure largely in another series of paintings. Armchair travelers could visit far-off places where life always seemed simpler and more rewarding, where hard work yielded sustenance and the forests grew green and lush. The consistent choice of images in Ruley's paintings suggest that his escapist fantasies often involved women—scantily clad and heavy with sexuality. Ruley himself often seems to peer from the canvas in the guise of a lion, a lynx, a steer.

Ellis Ruley absorbed the images disseminated by the

Figure 5. Photograph of Roy Rogers and Trigger. This *Life* magazine cover illustration from July 12, 1943, may have been the prototype for Ruley's painting *Lone Ranger* (Plate 18).

media, reassembled them, and returned them in a new form. His *Jungle Girl and Lion* (Plate 2) is clearly an adaptation of Henri Rousseau's painting *Le Rêve*, reproduced in *Life* magazine on September 11, 1950. His *Luau* (Plate 37) would seem to be based on stills from the 1950 M-G-M film *Pagan Love Song*, starring Howard Keel, Esther Williams, and Rita Moreno (figure 6). The ukulele-playing hero of this lighthearted painting is surrounded by a bevy of adoring saronged women. Again Ruley must have been attracted to a theme with interracial overtones. The character played by Keel

Figure 6. This M-G-M publicity photograph for the film *Pagan Love Song* was published in the New York *Daily News* on November 12, 1950. Ruley's painting *Luau* (Plate 37) reproduces this M-G-M photograph, perhaps depicting the artist's idealized dream of himself.

their hands. The resulting tableau is a pleasing geometric arrangement of the triangular ladder balanced by the ripe, round fruits that emphasize the female form.

While Ruley's paintings can be accepted on a superficial "pretty as a picture" basis, there is an underlying pathos that often disturbs the viewer. He relies faithfully on blithe, familiar images, but something has gone subtly awry. Beautiful girls flashing the toothy grins that sold products in the 1940s do not interact with either each other or the viewer (figure 8). They suggest a vacuousness hiding behind the smiles—beautiful, gay facades hiding empty promises. In *Accident* (Plate 11), the two girls smile incongruously as one is about to plunge into the depths of the lake. We are reminded, suddenly, of Ruley's isolated position in his community, where treacherous interactions took place behind a mask of civility.

In other paintings Ruley has slyly altered the nature of the scene with interjections of his own. Women seemingly become objects of fantasy, depicted with ear-to-ear smiles and spread legs. The curious *Circus* (Plate 40), in particular, may be suggestive of the artist's sexual longings. The female circus performer, wearing a bikini costume, lies along the length of an elephant's trunk which curls between her legs. Pointing at her figure with gleeful and seemingly implied sexual intent is a tiny clown holding a long, sharp object, half emerging from behind a tree. Tom Boyd, Professor of Philosophy at the University of Oklahoma, associates the clown with the outsider prototype: "resister, rebel, maverick, renegade, outlaw, visionary." Ruley could be portraying himself as the "innocent outsider," a clown, one of a group "neutralizing themselves by presenting themselves as outrageous." In this guise he would be at once "innocent and perverse," standing out while maintaining his individuality, freedom, and erotic thoughts behind the safety of the mask.

The "safety of the mask" appears in other instances, as well. Ruley peers through the eyes of the lynx, provoca-

falls madly in love with that played by Williams, whom he has mistaken for a Tahitian native. The promotional photograph echoed in Ruley's painting appeared in the *Daily News* Rotogravure Section on November 12, 1950, and circulated through Connecticut.

Sapping the Rubber Trees (Plate 21) and *First Steps to Finding Rubber* (Plate 10) may have been prompted by the February 1940 issue of *National Geographic*, a magazine that has consistently opened worlds and cultures to its readers through both photography and text. *Grapefruit Picking Time* (Plate 5) bears a strong similarity to photographs from the grapefruit and cherry festivals of the 1930s and '40s. Photographs of comely female pickers appeared in *Life* in June 1941 (figure 7). The women stood on different levels of a ladder opened in a fruit grove and held ripe fruit in

Figure 7. These "Cherry Queens, 1941" are shown in a photograph from *Life* magazine, June 2, 1941. Ruley was probably familiar with photographs of California fruit festivals which featured attractive women displaying fruit while posed in geometric formations.

Figure 8. Advertisement, Florida Citrus Commission (*Life* magazine, September 4, 1950). Advertisements such as this captured the bright, bouncy look popular in the 1950s. Ruley's *Accident* (Plate 11) seems to have been directly drawn from this illustration.

tively positioned above the nipple on the left breast of one of the two female figures in *Accident*. In *Daydreaming* (Plate 17), he seems to have assumed the guise of the lion, king of the jungle, basking in the adoration of his lioness. In *Eve* (Plate 36), his presence is merely implied, the voyeur who has startled a naked woman caught in the thick undergrowth and brambles of a forest.

In spite of his bravado, other paintings betray a sense of entrapment. Perhaps disguised once again as the lynx, Ruley occupies an ambivalent position in *Texes* [sic] *Bandits* (Plate 60). Though the rangers are hunting the bandits, Ruley as the lynx is forced into the role of witness from the precarious safety of a dark cave. His oversized figure dwarfs the scene around him, making his own discovery seem

unavoidable, though he is somewhat camouflaged by the coloration of the rocks around him. His mouth is open, ready to roar. But if he protects himself, ironically, he gives himself away. Perhaps this reflects Ruley's own struggle to live in a community in which his skin color and interracial marriage precluded anonymity.

This ambivalence is evident in other paintings which depict both hunters and the hunted. Yet Ruley's largest and most ambitious painting known, *Adam and Eve* (Plate 29), suggests his belief in a world where man and animal can coexist harmoniously. A seated Adam extends his left hand to the ripe apple. Eve, sitting on a rock opposite him, extends her right arm toward the apple, though her gaze is fixed on Adam. The central focus of the composition, the Tree of

Life—knowledge with its succulent fruit—exists without temptation or judgment; it just *is*. There are no hints of the consequences that will ensue when the snake surreptitiously descends from one of its branches. The pale, luminous figures are surrounded by full-bodied, peaceful animals—sheep and cows—that almost appear to be smiling. Around the bucolic scene is a stone gate, typical of those lining the Connecticut countryside where Ruley lived. The figure of Adam bears a marked resemblance to Ruley, while the general format and prepubescent body of Eve recall the work of sixteenth-century Dutch master Lucas Van Leyden and German master Lucas Cranach.

Ruley delves into the theme of unity even further in his original *Mothering Her Strange Calves* (Plate 55). A new twist on the traditional ugly duckling story, this intriguing painting pictures two fawns suckling from a cow who does not seem troubled by her "strange calves." The implication is one of brotherhood: we are all sisters and brothers. But there may be a deeper subtext suggested by parallels in Ruley's own life. The benign, proud look in the eyes of the steer glint with human intelligence. In fact, this would seem to be Ruley in disguise once again, beaming on his wife and children, while expressing an awareness of his neighbors' views of the Caucasian mother and her "strange," or interracial, calves.

Although it is not clear how Ruley became familiar with the work of artists such as those mentioned above, he evidently drew from academic as well as popular sources. His *Pieta* (Plate 34) is a direct adaptation of Adolphe William Bouguereau's study for *Premier Deuil* (figure 9). Bouguereau (1825–1905) was a popular French academic artist who painted classical and mythological subjects and treated them with almost photographic realism. The composition of Ruley's version of this painting is more complex than his other works, the bodies intertwining in a macabre death. Whether Ruley copied, traced, or transferred the image, forms were simplified in the process and details of the back-

Figure 9. *Premier Deuil* by Adolphe William Bouguereau (1825–1905) was auctioned at Sotheby's on October 29, 1992, lot 130. This composition is a direct source for Ruley's *Pieta* (Plate 34). Bouguereau was a popular nineteenth-century French academic artist who used optical realism to paint classical and mythological subjects.

ground eliminated. The legs atrophy into tiny, pointed feet while the arms terminate in solid, undefined hands. Ruley may have seen works such as this through his association with the Slater Museum in Norwich, the Wadsworth Atheneum in Hartford, or through reproductions in magazines, calendars, and other readily available sources. The fleshy, sensual, and romantic aspects of the classical style obviously appealed to Ellis Ruley. The use of an academic source is reminiscent of the earlier American tradition of portraiture based on the work of European court painters.

All of Ruley's paintings appear in outdoor settings. His need for freedom from enclosure and constraint is searingly evident, with fences occasionally intruding on open views of trees, sky, and water. Edenlike harmony is sought, but not always obtained. Ruley must have felt compelled to add notes of strife—animals fighting man and each other.

Little is known about Ellis Ruley's method of painting. He worked primarily with oil-based house paint on Masonite and posterboard and seems to have varnished the extant works. His subject matter is representational but rendered in simplified, flat forms, often outlined in pencil and filled in with color. Creases, shadows, and other modeling in the forms are also outlined and filled. The result is graphic and somehow true to the aesthetic of the popular sources he uses as a starting point for so many compositions.

The backgrounds of his paintings are composed of details and the repetitive use of pattern, broken by horizontal and vertical elements. Ruley apparently was not concerned with creating the illusion of three-dimensionality, nor inhibited by an adherence to a rational scheme of single perspective. Like the works of many self-taught artists, Ruley's paintings show several perspectives simultaneously, a visual device that provides maximum information to the viewer. The paintings also show two distinct approaches to color. One group of paintings is characterized by autumn tones—browns, greens, golds—and areas of high contrast. These same color schemes were prevalent in the late 1940s and early '50s: cocoa brown and hunter green walls were recommended in popular decorating magazines, and other self-taught artists of the period such as Horace Pippin also relied on this contemporary palette. A smaller body of Ruley's work was created in a monochromatic color scheme. This group includes some of the more lyrical paintings such as *Woman with Horse* (Plate 12), which seems to hark back to an earlier, more peaceful period. Ruley uses color effectively to set a mood. The purplish-blue face in *Girl Wading* (Plate 28) creates a mysterious quality that is echoed by deeper tones in the shadows; the chalky-white skin color of Adam and Eve underscores their otherworldly, spiritual aspect just at the moment before they succumb to temptation.

Decorative patterning—especially of leaves and blossoms—is another important feature of Ruley's paintings. The spots of color create a scintillating, pulsating surface in contrast to large unbroken areas of flat color. Confettilike colors add movement to otherwise static scenes, as though the figures have been caught in a moment of frozen animation. In 1943, *Life* magazine featured an advertisement by the Farnsworth Television Company (figure 10). The image shows a picture splitting into thousands of parts and cohering on a

Figure 10. Advertisement, Farnsworth Television Company (*Life* magazine, July 26, 1943). Ruley's confetti-strewn scenes are in tune with popular images of the period.

television set miles away. Ruley seems to have been sensitive to the winds of change, as new technology was just beginning to influence the way we look at the world around us.

Ellis Ruley's daily existence, as far as we know, gave little hint of the rich workings of his imagination. His paintings are a fascinating distillation of a bombardment of popular images filtered through the private yearnings, disappointments, and triumphs of one man's life. Ellis Ruley's paintings reveal knowledge not only about the artist but about the forces that subliminally shape all our lives. The lesson we learn is how to control those forces and refashion them into our own unique images.

—Stacy Hollander,
Curator, Museum of American Folk Art

—Lee Kogan,
Associate Director, Folk Art Institute
Senior Research Fellow,
Museum of American Folk Art

THE
PAINTINGS

PLATE 1. **GREENING KING BILLY AND THUNDER**

22" x 28", oil-based house paint on posterboard
Collection of John and Ann Ollman

PLATE 2. **JUNGLE GIRL AND LION**
22″ x 28″, oil-based house paint on posterboard
Collection of George H. Meyer

PLATE 3. **AUTUM [SIC] LEAVES**
28″ x 22″, oil-based house paint on posterboard
Courtesy of Glenn and Linda Smith

PLATE 4. **SPOOKED**
18½″ x 25″, oil-based house paint on Masonite
Private Collection

PLATE 5. **GRAPEFRUIT PICKING TIME**
31½″ x 25¼″, *oil-based house paint on posterboard*
The Amistad Foundation's African-American Collection at the Wadsworth Atheneum, Hartford, Connecticut

PLATE 6. **CHEIF [SIC] GREY OWL + WIFE**
28″ x 22″, oil-based house paint on posterboard
Private Collection

PLATE 7.   **MRS. GREY OWL AND HER PET BEAVER**
28" x 22", oil-based house paint on posterboard
Private Collection

PLATE 8. **UNTITLED (MAN LEAVING TRAIN)**
22˝ x 28˝, oil-based house paint on posterboard
Courtesy of Glenn and Linda Smith

PLATE 9. **JESSIE [sɪc] JAMES AND WIFE**
28″ x 22″, oil-based house paint on posterboard
Collection of Donald Levine

PLATE 10. **FIRST STEPS TO FINDING RUBBER**
31½″ x 25¼″, oil-based house paint on posterboard
The Amistad Foundation's African-American Collection at the Wadsworth Atheneum, Hartford, Connecticut

PLATE 11. **ACCIDENT**
22˝ x 28˝, oil-based house paint on posterboard
Collection of Chuck and Jan Rosenak

PLATE 12. **WOMAN WITH HORSE**
17¼″ x 22″, oil-based house paint on posterboard
Collection of Janet Fleisher Gallery

PLATE 13. **SOUTHMORE, TAKING A BATH WITH THE SENEORAS** [SIC]

28" x 22", oil-based house paint on posterboard
Courtesy of Glenn and Linda Smith

PLATE 14. **AUTUMN ON THE FARM**
23″ x 29½″, oil-based house paint on posterboard
Private Collection

PLATE 15. **CRUISING**
27½" x 22", oil-based house paint on posterboard
Collection of Robert and Nancy Claster

PLATE 16. **WILD PIG**
24″ x 20″, oil-based house paint on Masonite
Collection of George H. Meyer

PLATE 17. **DAYDREAMING**
28˝ x 22˝, oil-based house paint on posterboard
Collection of Slater Memorial Museum

PLATE 18. **LONE RANGER**
21½″ x 17″, oil-based house paint on posterboard
Private Collection

PLATE 19. **MCNOIL'S FAMOUS HORSE**
28″ x 22″, oil-based house paint on posterboard
Courtesy of Glenn and Linda Smith

PLATE 20. **HIPPOS**
30″ x 24″, oil-based house paint on Masonite
Collection of Janet Fleisher Gallery

PLATE 21. **SAPPING THE RUBBER TREES**

28″ x 22″, oil-based house paint on posterboard
Collection of Suzanne and Richard Barancik

PLATE 22. **MOOSE IN STREAM**
19˝ x 23˝, oil-based house paint on Academy board
Private Collection

PLATE 23. **THREE NUDE WOMEN IN A GARDEN**
31½″ x 25¼″, oil-based house paint on posterboard
The Amistad Foundation's African-American Collection at the Wadsworth Atheneum, Hartford, Connecticut

PLATE 24. **SWIMMING POOL**
27½″ x 22″, oil-based house paint on posterboard
Collection of Janet Fleisher Gallery

PLATE 25. **STAG HUNT**
28″x 22″, oil-based house paint on posterboard
Private Collection

PLATE 26. **WATERFALL**
28" x 22", oil-based house paint on posterboard
Collection of Suzanne and Richard Barancik

PLATE 27. **LAKES A LEAP**
28˝ x 22˝, oil-based house paint on posterboard
Private Collection

PLATE 28. **GIRL WADING**
26½″ x 19½″, oil-based house paint on posterboard
Courtesy of Jacqueline and Malcolm Pryor

PLATE 29. **ADAM AND EVE**

39″ x 43″, oil-based house paint on Masonite
Courtesy of Glenn and Linda Smith

PLATE 30. **DUDE RANCH**

28″ x 22″, oil-based house paint on posterboard
Private Collection

PLATE 31. **BEAUTY AND FLOWER**
18″ x 25″, oil-based house paint on Masonite
Private Collection

PLATE 32. **PITTSFIELD STATE FORREST [SIC]—SEE HOW PRETTY**
28˝ x 22˝, oil-based house paint on posterboard
Private Collection

PLATE 33. **JUNGLE GIRL**
27½" x 22", oil-based house paint on posterboard
Collection of John and Nancy Hellebrand

PLATE 34. **PIETA**
24″ x 30″, oil-based house paint on posterboard
Collection of Janet Fleisher Gallery

PLATE 35. **MYTH**
18″ x 24½″, oil-based house paint on posterboard
Collection of Janet Fleisher Gallery

PLATE 36. **EVE**
29½˝ x 23½˝, oil-based house paint on Masonite
Blumert/Fiore Collection

PLATE 37. **LUAU**
21½″ x 28″, oil-based house paint on posterboard
Collection of Anne and Monty Blanchard, courtesy of Cavin-Morris Gallery

PLATE 38. **ZEBRAS**
22″ x 28″, oil-based house paint on posterboard
Courtesy of Pompei Olivia

PLATE 39. **ENGLAND**
22" x 26½", oil-based house paint on posterboard
Collection of Jill and Sheldon Bonovitz

PLATE 40. **CIRCUS**
28″ x 22″, oil-based house paint on posterboard
Private Collection

PLATE 41. **SHEEP**
22″ x 28″, oil-based house paint on posterboard
Collection of Mario Gualtieri

PLATE 42. **CHEIF [SIC] GREY OWL AND WIFE**

22" x 28", oil-based house paint on posterboard
Collection of George H. Meyer

PLATE 43. **MOOSE**
25½″ x 21½″, oil-based house paint on posterboard
Private Collection

PLATE 44. **DAY OF SPORT**
28" x 22", oil-based house paint on posterboard
Collection of Janet Fleisher Gallery

PLATE 45. **TIGER ATTACKING MAN**
19½″ x 23″, oil-based house paint on Masonite
Collection of Janet Fleisher Gallery

PLATE 46. **MOOSE IN BATTLE**
20½″ x 24″, oil-based house paint on Masonite
Collection of Janet Fleisher Gallery

PLATE 47. **PARROT GIRL**
28″ x 22″, oil-based house paint on posterboard
Collection of Chuck and Jan Rosenak

PLATE 48. **PUMPKIN HARVEST**
22" x 28", oil-based house paint on posterboard
Collection of George H. Meyer

PLATE 49. **TIGER**
18″ x 24½″, oil-based house paint on Masonite
Private Collection

PLATE 50. **A DAY OF HUNTING**
28″ x 22″, oil-based house paint on posterboard
Collection of George H. Meyer

PLATE 51. **GOING TO LAY THEM OUT**
28″ x 22″, oil-based house paint on posterboard
Collection of Herbert Waide Hemphill, Jr.

PLATE 52.   **CHERRY BLOSSUM [sic] TIME**
28˝ x 22˝, oil-based house paint on posterboard
Private Collection

PLATE 53. **TRAPPED STAG**
20˝ x 17˝, oil-based house paint on posterboard
Collection of George H. Meyer

PLATE 54. **WATERFALL WITH BRIDE**
28¼″ x 22″, oil-based house paint on posterboard
Collection of Laura C. Levine

PLATE 55. **MOTHERING HER STRANGE CALVES**
22″ x 28″, oil-based house paint on posterboard
Collection of Didi and David Barrett, Saralee and Paul Pincus

PLATE 56. **A COUNTRY BARN**
21˝ x 27˝, oil-based house paint on posterboard
Collection of Elizabeth Felding Radoff

PLATE 57. **A COUNTRY FARM SCENE**
21˝ x 27˝, oil-based house paint on posterboard
Collection of Elizabeth Felding Radoff

PLATE 58. **CHERRY BLOSSUM [SIC] TIME**
21˝ x 27˝, oil-based house paint on posterboard
Private Collection

PLATE 59. **HUNTING STAGS**
20" x 24", oil-based house paint on Masonite
Private Collection

PLATE 60. **TEXES** [SIC] **BANDITS**
28″x 22″, oil-based house paint on posterboard
Courtesy of Fred and Kathryn Giampietro

PLATE 61. **PHEASANT**
28″ x 22″, oil-based house paint on posterboard
Collection of John Lee and Joanne Brown Lee

PLATE 62. **PARROT GIRL**
28″ x 22″, oil-based house paint on posterboard
Private Collection